Polar bears live here.
Polar bears have to stay warm.

3

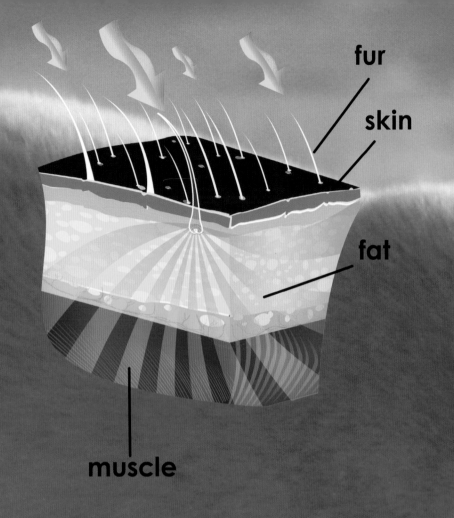

fur

skin

fat

muscle

Their fat keeps them warm.
They have to stay fat so
that they can stay warm.

4

Polar bears have to eat
lots of food to stay fat.

Polar bears eat seals.

Seals swim in the water.
They can swim very fast.

Polar bears can swim, but they can't swim as fast as seals can!

This makes it hard for polar bears to catch seals in the water. So polar bears hunt for seals on the ice.

This polar bear is going to hunt for a seal on the ice.

She will look for a hole in the ice. She could walk for a long time before she finds one.

The polar bear will use her nose to find a hole.

When she finds a hole,
she will sit and wait for
the seal to show up.

The seal swims under the ice.
He has to come up for air.
He will use the hole in the ice
to come up for air.

14

The seal puts his head up
into the hole. He opens
his mouth to get air.

The polar bear smells the seal's breath.

She puts her paw into
the hole. She grabs the
seal out of the water.

17

She pulls the seal onto
the ice. She kills the seal
with her claws and her
teeth. Now she can eat.

18

This is how a polar bear hunts seals.

POLAR BEAR
ANATOMY

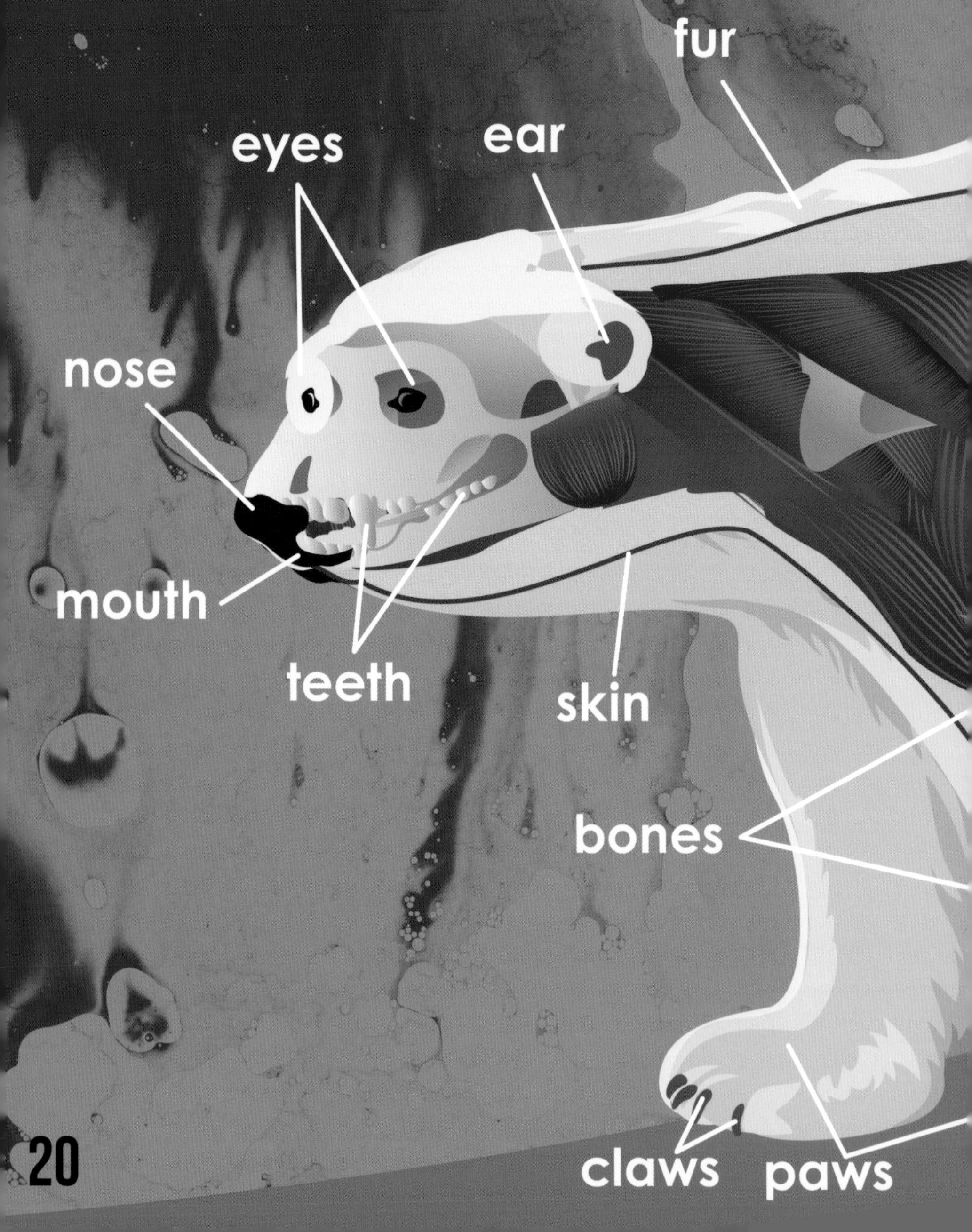

fur

eyes   ear

nose

mouth

teeth

skin

bones

claws   paws

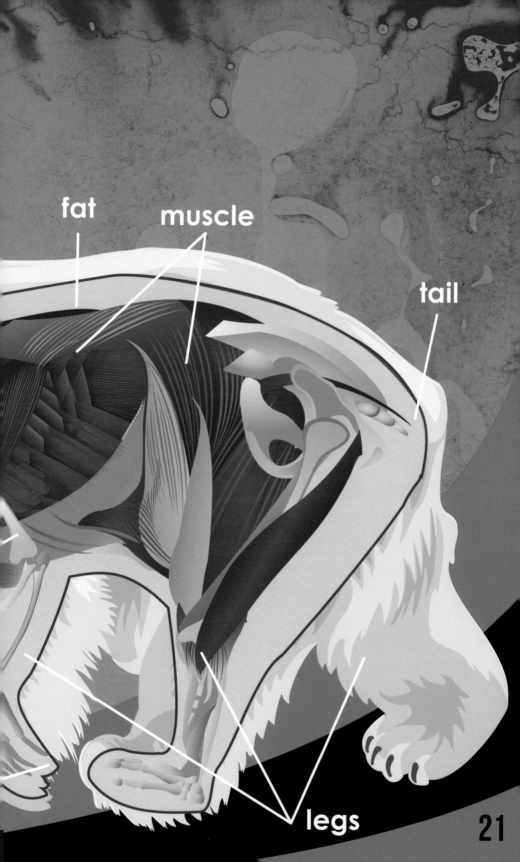

fat

muscle

tail

legs

21

USE THE WORDS YOU
KNOW
TO READ NEW WORDS!

saw	**it**
raw	hit
paw	kit
claw	sit
see	**play**
bee	lay
beep	say
keep	stay

at	**him**
sat	Tim
rat	trim
fat	swim

too	**fun**
zoo	sun
mood	hunt
food	hunts

will	**ar**
fill	car
hill	hard
kill	warm

23

TRICKY WORDS

before

catch

find

long

pull

very

walk